Celebrating 24 years of
Mick & Brita

The publishers and authors would like to thank Robert Davies
of the British Library for his invaluable assistance.

Published in the U.K. by Otter-Barry Books as
Books! Books! Books!: Explore Inside the Greatest Library on Earth
First U.S. edition 2017

Library of Congress Catalog Card Number pending
ISBN 978-0-7636-9757-0

17 18 19 20 21 22 TLF 10 9 8 7 6 5 4 3 2 1

Printed in Dongguan, Guangdong, China

This book was typeset in ITC American Typewriter.
The illustrations were done in watercolor and digital art.

Candlewick Press
99 Dover Street
Somerville, Massachusetts 02144

visit us at www.candlewick.com

BOOKS! BOOKS! BOOKS!

MICK MANNING & BRITA GRANSTRÖM

Explore the
AMAZING
Collection of the
BRITISH LIBRARY

CANDLEWICK PRESS

CONTENTS

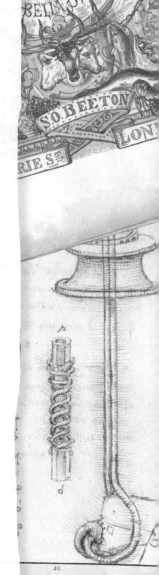

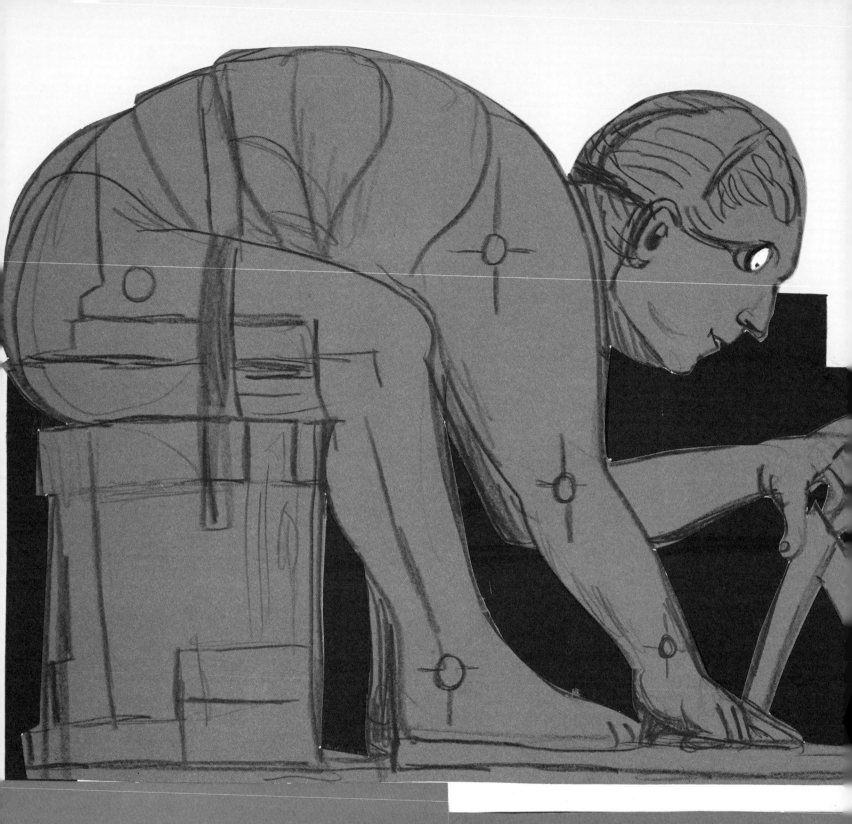

WELCOME to the greatest library in the world! We're going to take you on an amazing tour of its treasures—including some that are so rare they are kept under lock and key!

Welcome

The British Library, in London, is the national library of the United Kingdom and the largest public building constructed in the U.K. in the twentieth century. It was built between 1988 and 1998, using ten million bricks and 180,000 tons of concrete. Inside it has 400 miles/625 kilometers of shelves! And when you stand on the ground floor, there are nine floors above your head and five floors beneath your feet. **It's a giant**—just like Eduardo Paolozzi's sculpture of famous scientist Isaac Newton in the courtyard.

The British Library holds one of the largest collections of books, prints, letters, drawings, maps, stamps, newspapers, plays, and music in the world—more than 150 million items, from the earliest printed books to books printed this year. So the British Library collection is a unique history of the book.

Are you ready to go inside?

Let's begin at the beginning, with
ancient handmade books like
THE St. CUTHBERT GOSPEL,
found in a coffin!

The Gospel was originally placed in Saint Cuthbert's coffin at Lindisfarne Priory, in Northumberland, some time after his death, in 687 CE.

Later, it traveled with the saint's body as it was moved around the north of England to avoid the invading Vikings. The coffin was finally buried in Durham Cathedral.

The saint's Gospel was taken out of the coffin in the 1100s and later fell into private hands—until the British Library bought it, in 2011, for nine million pounds!

The St. Cuthbert Gospel, which contains the Gospel of Saint John, is the oldest surviving book produced in Europe to have its original covers and binding.

cepi⸱ ˑuˈ noᴍo ᴍιssus aᴅo
ᴀтιᴀ⸱ᴦ cuι noᴍєn єʀᴀт ιoʜᴀnnєs

And look at this: the magnificent
Lindisfarne Gospels,
hand-lettered and painted by a monk
named Eadfrith more than thirteen
hundred years ago.

This beautiful book, containing all four
Gospels, is presumed to be the work of
Eadfrith, Bishop of Lindisfarne, a gifted
artist and scribe. It was made around
700 CE in honor of Saint Cuthbert.
The original cover, decorated with jewels,
was stolen by Viking raiders.

Then there are stories about some of the earliest superheroes, like the Swedish warrior **BEOWULF**—a hero so strong, he tore off a man-eating monster's arm in single combat!

Beowulf comes to help a Danish king, whose men are being attacked by a man-eating monster known as Grendel.

Beowulf lies in wait for Grendel and, in a brutal wrestling match, tears off the monster's arm. Grendel flees, bleeding to death.

Grendel's mother is even fiercer! But Beowulf tracks her to the bottom of a lake and kills her with a sword.

Beowulf is the oldest surviving long poem in Old English. The British Library's copy, three thousand lines long, was hand-written in the eleventh century. Set in Scandinavia and brought to Britain by Anglo-Saxon settlers, the poem is a thrilling adventure story that was originally told out loud at feasts and gatherings.

Here is the famous Magna Carta, a historic promise to be just and fair, sealed by King John of England.

The Magna Carta became an important part of English law, and laws in the U.K. today are still based on it. When the United States won independence from Britain, the Magna Carta influenced the U.S. Constitution and its Bill of Rights.

English nobles became fed up with King John's unfair punishments, heavy taxes, and land grabbing to raise money for a war he was losing in France. So they decided to rebel.

To avoid a rebellion, a legal document was drawn up to say what the king could and could not do. *Magna Carta* means "Great Charter," and it was sealed, unwillingly, by King John in 1215 at Runnymede, beside the river Thames.

And here is
The Canterbury Tales,
by Geoffrey Chaucer, the first book ever printed in English, using an amazing invention: movable type and a printing press!

Until the fifteenth century, all books in Europe were handwritten, usually in Latin, but in 1436, the printing press was invented in Germany. William Caxton brought one to Britain in 1476, and with it he printed *The Canterbury Tales*, a collection of entertaining stories about a group of pilgrims traveling to Canterbury Cathedral. Shown above is a picture from "The Knight's Tale," the story of two brave and honorable knights who fall in love with the same lady and fight a courtly duel to decide who will marry her.

There are **BIG** books, like this
ginormous atlas made for King Charles
the Second, THE KLENCKE ATLAS.
It's so heavy, it takes six people to lift it!

This book of maps was printed in Holland and presented to King Charles II in 1660. It has thirty-seven maps showing all parts of the world known to Europeans at that time, and when opened, it measures 7 feet × 5 feet 10 inches/ 2.1 × 1.78 meters!

VA DESCRITTIONE D'ITALIA DI GIOANN. ANTONIO MAGINO.

And there are tiny books such as
Lady Jane Grey's Prayer Book.
It might make you feel sad.

Lady Jane Grey was a great-niece of Henry VIII. She became queen of England at the age of seventeen but ruled for only nine days before Henry's daughter Mary took power. Jane was imprisoned and sentenced to death. She carried this little handwritten book to her execution, and it even has some of her own scribbled messages in the margins. The book measures just 2¾ × 3⅜ inches/70 × 85 millimeters.

Some books in the British Library, such as the First Folio of **𝔚illiam 𝔖hakespeare,** are so valuable that they are kept in bombproof strong rooms, deep underground.

The graveyard scene from *Hamlet*

Alas, poor Yorick!

William Shakespeare grew up in the age of Queen Elizabeth I. As a young man, he left his hometown of Stratford-upon-Avon to work in the new theaters that were springing up in London. Shakespeare went on to become the world's greatest dramatist, writing many unforgettable plays, including *Romeo and Juliet*, *A Midsummer Night's Dream*, *Hamlet*, and *Macbeth*.

The balcony scene from *Romeo and Juliet*

O, speak again, bright angel!

The First Folio, the first full collection of Shakespeare's plays, was printed in 1623. Eighteen of the thirty-six plays had never been published before, so without the First Folio, some of the finest plays in the world might have been lost forever.

TOFFEE, RUSSIAN.

INGREDIENTS.—¾ of a lb. of loaf sugar, ¼ of a pint of cream, flavouring.

METHOD.—Dissolve the sugar in the cream, stand the stewpan in a bain-marie or tin of boiling water, and stir and cook until the mixture thickens and leaves the sides of the pan. Remove from the fire, stir in the flavouring essence, pour on to oiled or greased tins, and when cold cut into squares.

Are you hungry after all that drama? In the mood for some cod shoulder or sheep's head? There are enough COOKBOOKS in the British Library to give you a serious tummy ache!

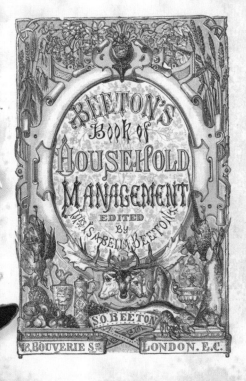

From medieval recipes to cookbooks by modern TV celebrities, the shelves of the British Library contain the whole history of British cooking and eating. You can find recipes to create a fourteenth-century dinner or discover that English children drank beer for breakfast in the 1600s.

Mrs. Isabella Beeton was the superstar cookbook writer of Victorian times. Her *Book of Household Management*, a huge bestseller, was published in 1861. More than just a cookbook, it also gives advice on everything from cleaning silver to getting rid of rats!

Still have a tummy ache? Well, there are MEDICAL BOOKS, too—but some of the older ones in the British Library's collection might make you feel even worse!

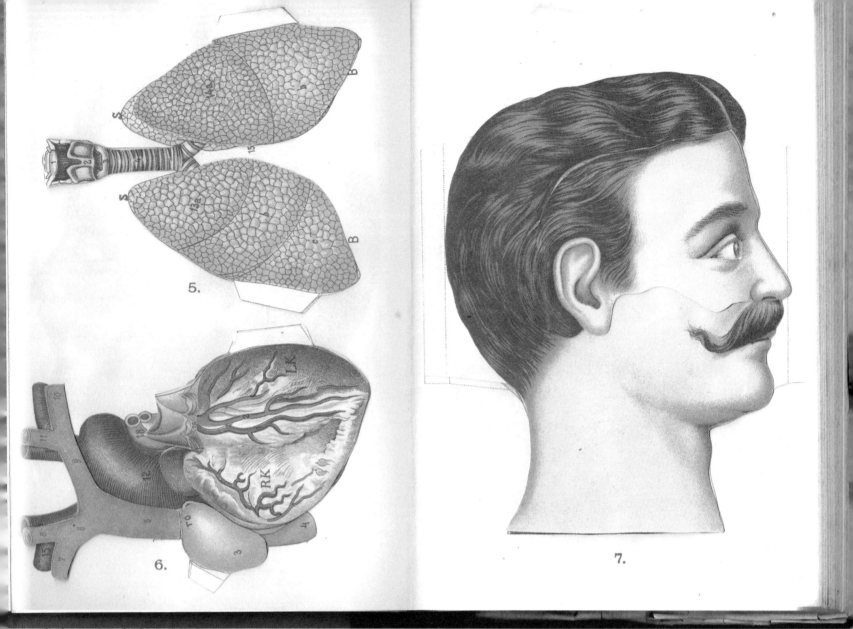

5.

6.

7.

People come from all over the world to the British Library to find some of the best— as well as the strangest—books on medicine. A Scottish doctor in the eighteenth century, Charles Alston, described how the juice of squashed wood lice could be used to cure children's colic, in his book *Lectures on the Materia Medica* (1770).

The New Natural Healing Method, by the pioneering nineteenth-century doctor Friedrich Bilz, features amazing foldouts and paper engineering.

Look out for the works of such great women writers as *Jane Austen,* who wrote witty, clever books about love, pride, and jealousy among the English gentry.

Jane Austen wrote her stories in the early 1800s. Her six wonderful novels are full of lively characters, intrigues, and romances, from *Sense and Sensibility,* about two sisters seeking love in very different ways, to *Emma,* a funny and touching story about a headstrong girl who tries unsuccessfully to do some matchmaking for her friend!

Here is fifteen-year-old Jane Austen writing her *History of England,* which makes fun of the usual kind of boring history books that children had to read in those days. Jane's sister, Cassandra, drew the pictures.

PRIDE & PREJUDICE

by JANE AUSTEN

With twenty-four coloured illustrations
by C. E. BROCK

In Jane Austen's most famous story, *Pride and Prejudice,* we meet Mr. Darcy, the arrogant upper-class gentleman who learns he has been too proud, and Elizabeth Bennet, the clever girl with whom he falls in love—along with the rest of the Bennet sisters and their comic, foolish mother—plus a villainous soldier!

Elizabeth Bennet first sees proud Mr. Darcy at a ball.

Mr. Darcy finally reveals a secret to Elizabeth, which shows his true character.

And let's look at the handwritten stories, letters, and novels of the three extraordinary **Brontë sisters,** who lived and wrote in a parsonage on the wild Yorkshire moors almost two hundred years ago.

Emily Brontë's *Wuthering Heights,* set on the moors, tells a dramatic story of violence and passion between Cathy and Heathcliff.

Charlotte Brontë's *Jane Eyre* shows how Jane survives harsh school days to become an independent young woman who, as a governess, falls in love with her boss, Mr. Rochester.

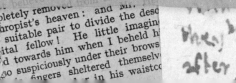

Anne Brontë's *The Tenant of Wildfell Hall* is about a married woman brave enough to leave her dissolute husband and take her child with her.

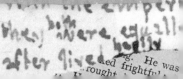

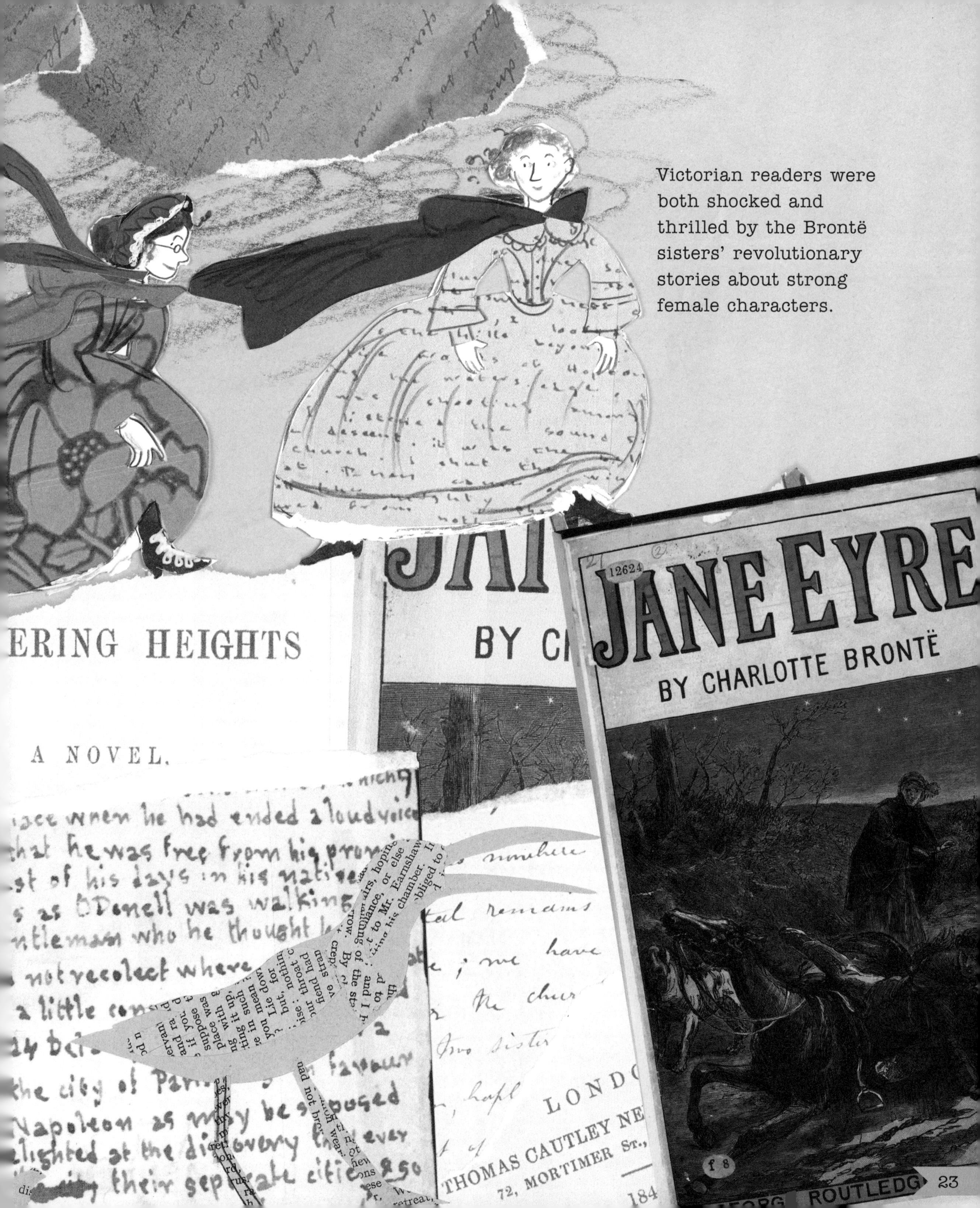

Victorian readers were both shocked and thrilled by the Brontë sisters' revolutionary stories about strong female characters.

ERING HEIGHTS

A NOVEL.

JANE EYRE

BY CHARLOTTE BRONTË

12624

LONDON

THOMAS CAUTLEY NE

72, MORTIMER ST.,

184

GEORG ROUTLEDG

And there are books by brothers, too.
THE BROTHERS GRIMM roamed
Germany two hundred years ago, looking for
tales of wicked witches and cruel queens.

Brothers Wilhelm and Jakob Grimm collected word-of-mouth fairy tales such as "Hansel and Gretel," "Snow White," and "Rapunzel" from country folk and wrote them down. Without the books of the Brothers Grimm, these magical stories could have been forgotten and lost forever.

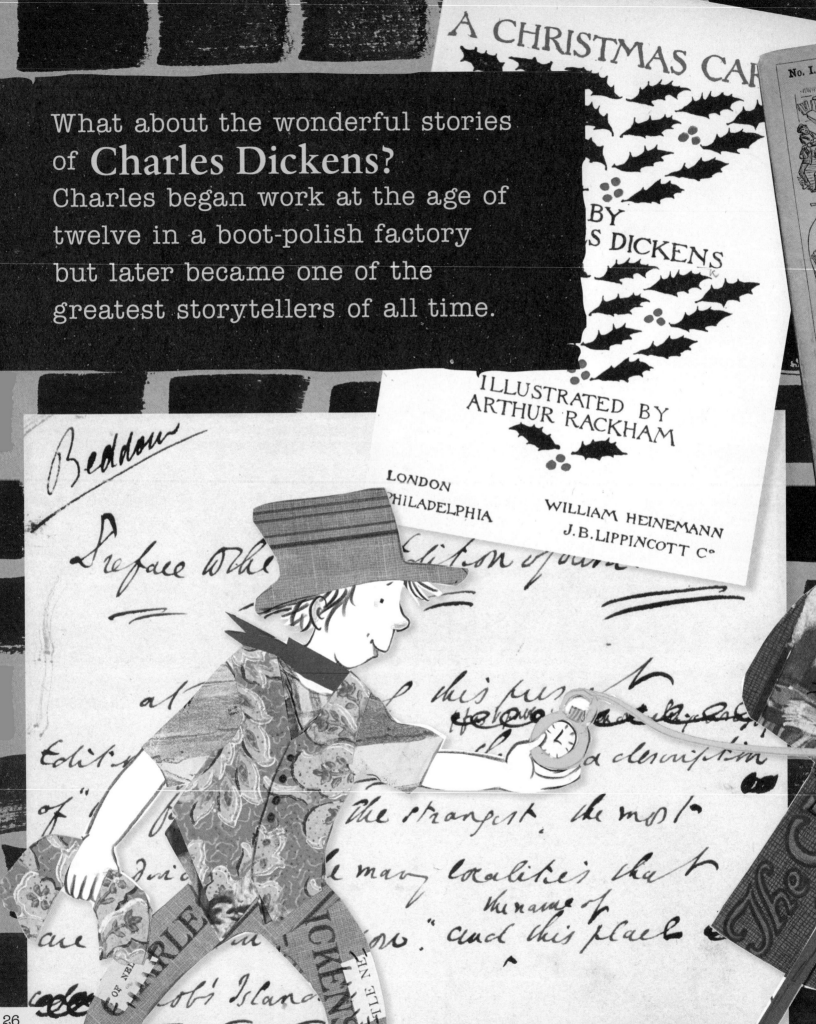

What about the wonderful stories of **Charles Dickens?**
Charles began work at the age of twelve in a boot-polish factory but later became one of the greatest storytellers of all time.

Charles Dickens's many novels, all written in the nineteenth century, championed the poor and homeless and were a voice against child labor. In *Oliver Twist*, a poor orphan gets caught up in a criminal gang, and in *The Old Curiosity Shop*, Little Nell and her grandpa have to leave their beloved shop and become homeless beggars.

When poor Oliver Twist asks for more gruel in the workhouse, he is cruelly punished.

Little Nell and her grandpa have to say good-bye to their home, the Old Curiosity Shop, forever.

But the
British Library
doesn't just boast great
storytellers. It proudly
celebrates the greatest scientific
minds of all time, too, with
treasures like the notebooks
of the artist and inventor
*Leonardo
da Vinci.*

This collection of drawings and notes shows us the workings of Leonardo's amazing and ambitious mind. He lived in the fifteenth century, but even now his designs are helping scientists develop machines to be used in possible future landings on Mars!

Leonardo wrote backward in his notebooks, maybe to keep them secret but more likely because he could and found it funny!

And there are nature books, like this one by the eighteenth-century writer Oliver Goldsmith.

Of course the genius **Charles Darwin** is here, too. His five-year voyage around the world led him to make tremendous discoveries about evolution, which he wrote about in his 1859 masterwork, *On the Origin of Species*.

Oliver Goldsmith's hugely popular *A History of the Earth, and Animated Nature*, first published in 1774, was republished in 1824, illustrated with many beautiful engravings.

Darwin was inspired to write *On the Origin of Species* after his five-year world voyage as a young scientist aboard HMS *Beagle*. The book challenged the traditional view of how the world was created, with discoveries about how animal species had evolved over time, including the revolutionary idea that humans are descended from apes.

After all that science, what about something very unscientific—Lewis Carroll's unforgettable story of a little girl named Alice who falls down a rabbit hole and discovers a magical world . . .

Alice's Adventures in Wonderland.

ALICE'S ADVENTURES IN WONDERLAND

Alice's Adventures in Wonderland is about a little girl who shrinks and travels to the weird and fantastic world of Wonderland, where she meets a White Rabbit, a sleepy Dormouse, a Mad Hatter, a crazy Queen of Hearts, and lots of other amazing characters. It was published in 1865 and not only changed the way many people thought about children's books but was read by many adults, too.

In Won

If you prefer facts to fantasy, catch up on the news with more than sixty million **NEWSPAPERS**— including the first ever copy of London's the *Times*.

The *Times* was first printed in 1788. Alongside politics and news about the trials of highwaymen, there were theater and opera announcements and lots of advertisements. Can you spot the ad for a book about horse-riding skills? In the eighteenth century that was the equivalent of learning to drive a car!

Or how about a concert with handwritten sheet music to make you sing and dance? This is the explosive *Music for the Royal Fireworks* by Handel.

Handel could erupt like a firework himself. His rages were famous. Once he threw a kettledrum at the leader of an orchestra so hard that his wig fell off in the effort.

George Frideric Handel's *Music for the Royal Fireworks* was first performed in the open air, in London, in 1749. Handel's handwritten score is part of the British Library's vast music collection, which includes works by thousands of world-famous composers.

THE HOUND
OF THE
BASKERVILLES

A.G.J.

CONAN DOYLE

Feeling tired after all that? How about an adventure story before bedtime? Join the super-sleuth SHERLOCK HOLMES and his faithful friend, Dr. Watson, as they track down the Hound of the Baskervilles.

Sir Arthur Conan Doyle is most famous for his renowned series of detective adventures featuring the eccentric genius Sherlock Holmes and his loyal sidekick, Dr. Watson.

In *The Hound of the Baskervilles*, published in 1902, Holmes and Watson try to solve a terrifying mystery on lonely Dartmoor. Not only is an escaped prisoner on the loose but a giant, savage dog is terrorizing the moor!

We hope you enjoyed your tour of the BRITISH LIBRARY and some of its treasures. The library receives a copy of every single book published in the United Kingdom and Ireland—including this one! When you order a book from the collection to look at, it travels to you from the vaults on an automatic conveyor system, like a little railway. Find out about British Library events and exhibitions at www.bl.uk.

Almost every country in the world has a national library. The Library of Congress in Washington, D.C., claims to be the largest of all. Founded in 1800, it holds more than 162 million items. Australia's National Library, in Canberra, is much younger, founded in 1960, but already has more than ten million items. However, libraries don't have to be huge to have great books. Perhaps there is a public lending library near you. Go and support your local libraries, and see for yourself what exciting places they are.

MORE ABOUT THE WORKS AND THEIR AUTHORS

THE ST. CUTHBERT GOSPEL: This book, which contains the Gospel of John, is tiny, 3½ × 5½ inches/92 × 138 millimeters. It is handwritten in Latin, in beautiful script.

THE LINDISFARNE GOSPELS: This book was written and painted on vellum (calfskin) and contains the Gospels of Matthew, Mark, Luke, and John. The picture on page 5 is from the Gospel of John.

BEOWULF: The copy in the British Library is unique and so extremely fragile that it has to be looked after very carefully in case it crumbles away.

THE MAGNA CARTA: The other earliest copies of this historic legal agreement are kept at Salisbury and Lincoln Cathedrals.

GEOFFREY CHAUCER: Chaucer was a royal courtier and a diplomat. His groundbreaking books were so important that he became known as the father of English literature and influenced future writers like William Shakespeare.

THE KLENCKE ATLAS: This was the largest atlas in the world until 2012, when an even larger atlas, entitled *Earth Platinum,* was created in Australia.

LADY JANE GREY'S PRAYER BOOK: Small personal books of prayers were often created for wealthy people so they could carry them wherever they went.

COOKBOOKS: The oldest known cookbook in English is *The Forme of Cury* (*The Method Cooking*), handwritten around 1390, with recipes used in the royal kitchen. The British Library has the first printed copy, published in 1780.

MEDICAL BOOKS: The British Library has works by some of the great forerunners of modern medicine, including Edward Jenner (1749–1823), who coined the word *vaccine* for his smallpox inoculations; Sir James Young Simpson (1811–1870), pioneer of anesthetics; and Joseph Lister (1827–1912), who introduced antiseptic methods in surgery. These discoveries have saved millions of lives.

WILLIAM SHAKESPEARE: The British Library has five precious copies of the First Folio. Out of the 750 copies printed, there are thought to be only 233 surviving today.

JANE AUSTEN: Though she was one of the greatest romantic novelists, Austen never married. She did, however, become engaged—for just twenty-four hours. She changed her mind the next day and refused her suitor.

THE BRONTË SISTERS: The Brontë sisters first published their novels under different names so that the publishers and readers would not know they were women. Anne was Acton Bell, Emily was Ellis Bell, and Charlotte was Currer Bell. But as their books became bestsellers, the sisters revealed their true identities.

THE BROTHERS GRIMM: The Grimms' first fairy-tale collection, *Children's and Household Tales,* was published in 1812. However, the fairy tales the brothers wrote down were not originally told for children. They were told out loud to grown-ups, and they could be frightening.

CHARLES DICKENS: Many of Dickens's novels first appeared as serialized chapters, sold in monthly installments. They were hugely popular, and people couldn't wait to buy the next episode.

LEONARDO DA VINCI: Leonardo was one of the great artists of his time. His famous portrait *The Mona Lisa,* on display at the Louvre, in Paris, is still the most valuable painting in the world.

OLIVER GOLDSMITH: Goldsmith wrote on many topics, but he is best known now as a playwright and as the author of the 1766 novel *The Vicar of Wakefield.*

CHARLES DARWIN: *On the Origin of Species* rocked the world with its explanation of how life has gradually evolved on our planet over millions of years.

ALICE'S ADVENTURES IN WONDERLAND: There are millions of copies of the Alice books in the world, but the British Library has Lewis Carroll's original manuscript, with his own sketches and notes. The tea party illustration on pages 32–33 is by Alice's most famous illustrator, John Tenniel.

NEWSPAPERS: The British Library has a copy of every newspaper published every day in Britain and Ireland since 1869, as well as many more going back to the seventeenth century.

GEORGE FRIDERIC HANDEL: Handel composed operas and oratorios (including *Messiah,* often performed at Christmastime) as well as his famous orchestral music. The music of many other great composers is also kept at the British Library.

SHERLOCK HOLMES: Sir Arthur Conan Doyle created many adventures for Sherlock Holmes. The British Library has first editions of them all.

GLOSSARY

ATLAS — a book of world maps

BRITISH LIBRARY — the U.K.'s national collection of books and manuscripts

CHARTER — an agreement in writing between two sets of people, saying what they promise to do for each other

CONSTITUTION — a set of rules that guides how a country or state works

EXECUTION — the act of being put to death as punishment for a crime

FOLIO — a book made by folding individual sheets of paper only once; can also be used to refer to a large-format book

GENTRY — a name traditionally given to people from families of high social standing, who were often rich and owned land or estates

GOSPELS — the four descriptions of the life and death of Jesus, by Saints Matthew, Mark, Luke, and John, in the New Testament of the Bible

MOVABLE TYPE — individual letters of the alphabet that can be fitted together to make words and sentences, then inked and pressed onto paper using a printing press

NOVEL — a long, entertaining, made-up story, usually featuring imaginary people and events

OLD ENGLISH — the language written and spoken by the Anglo-Saxons up to about 1100

REVOLUTIONARY — used to describe something that changes the way we live or think

SEAL — a special mark, made in soft wax that then hardens, used by only one person, such as a king, to show that the sealed item comes from him or her

SHEET MUSIC — handwritten or printed music that shows the melodies, rhythms, and chords of a musical piece

SLEUTH — another name for a detective, someone who solves criminal mysteries

IMAGE CREDITS